A Coronation is very special, somethi[ng] remember all your life. I hope this boo[k] you celebrate the occasion.

JEFF LINK, April 2023.

CONTENTS

NORFOLK
NN
NUGGETS
BOOKS

The King and Queen

The Coronation is a special ceremony where the King and Queen are crowned. Over the last 100 years there have only been 3 coronations, and it is over 70 years since the last coronation took place. That was when Elizabeth II, King Charles III's Mother, was crowned Queen.

On Saturday 6th May, 2023, The King and Queen Consort will ride in the Jubilee State Coach to Westminster Abbey to be crowned as King and Queen by the Archbishop of Canterbury.

The King will give a promise to serve his people and he will be anointed with oil. The Holy Oil is made from olives from two groves on the Mount of Olives, near the Old City of Jerusalem.

Monarchs often sit for several portraits during their reign. These may be photographs or paintings. On this page you can colour a portrait of King Charles III and Queen Camilla.

FUN FACT: a special dish was invented for Queen Elizabeth II's Coronation in 1953. It was called 'Coronation Chicken'.

King Charles III has chosen 'Coronation Quiche', made with eggs, cheese, spinach, tarragon and broad beans as his special dish.

Regalia - Ampulla, Spoon and Royal Orb

In addition to the Royal Crowns, other special historic objects will be used at the Coronation. These special objects are known as the Coronation Regalia; there are swords, sceptres, an orb and a special spoon.

Three items of Regalia are illustrated here. They are the Ampulla, which holds the anointing oil, the spoon for the oil and the golden orb.

The Holy oil which is also know as the 'Chrism' oil, is used to anoint the King. It's carried in an eagle shaped vessel which is called the ampulla, which is made of gold and is nearly 400 years old.

The Archbishop of Canterbury pours the oil onto the Coronation Spoon, which is also made of gold. It is the oldest object that will be used at the Coronation, and dates back to the medieval era.

FUN FACT: when the oil is poured, it comes out of the eagle's beak.

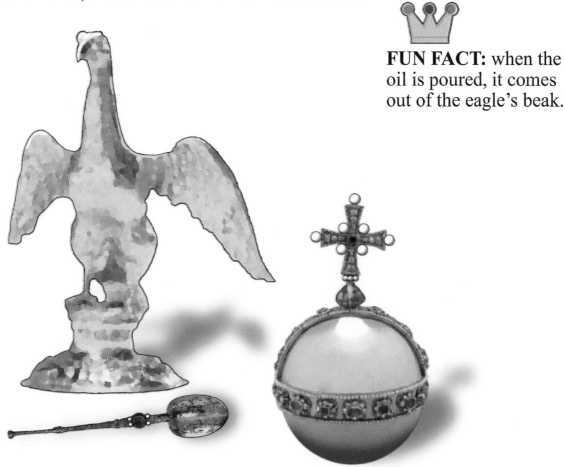

ILLUSTRATION: The Ampulla, Coronation Spoon and Royal Orb.

Regalia - Two Sceptres

A sceptre is a staff or rod held in the hand by a ruling monarch as an item of royal or imperial insignia, signifying sovereign authority.

King Charles will hold two sceptres. They are the Sceptre with Cross and the Sceptre with Dove.

The rods are made of gold, one has an enamelled heart-shaped structure which holds the Cullinan I diamond, the largest clear cut diamond in the world.

The other sceptre has a white dove on the top. This sceptre represents the Sovereign's spiritual role, with the dove representing the Holy Ghost. Traditionally it has been known as 'the Rod of Equity and Mercy'.

ILLUSTRATION: two sceptres, with close-up detail of the Sceptre with Cross and Sceptre with Dove.

Regalia - Two Royal Crowns

St. Edward's Crown. This Crown has been used at every Coronation since 1661. Created for Charles II, the crown is named after Edward the Confessor. It weighs nearly 5 lbs (2.23 kg), and is 12 inches tall (30.4 cm).

It is made from solid gold set with 444 gems rubies, amethysts and sapphires over a velvet cap.

Imperial State Crown. This is the Monarch's working crown and is used for formal occasions like the state opening of Parliament. It was made in 1937.

It has a purple velvet cap and is set with 2,868 diamonds, 17 sapphires, 11 emeralds and 269 pearls.

It is said the big ruby at the front of the crown, once belonged to King Henry V and he wore it on his helmet as he rode into the Battle of Agincourt in 1415.

FUN FACT: in order to wear such a heavy crown it is rumoured Queen Elizabeth II had to practice by wearing a bag of flour on her head.

ILLUSTRATION: St. Edward's Crown and the Imperial State Crown. Cut-out versions of these two Royal Crowns are on pages 7 and 9, for you to use creatively.

The Coronation Chair

The Coronation Chair has been used to crown Kings and Queens of the United Kingdom for over 700 years. The chair is also known as St. Edward's Chair or King Edward's Chair.

During the Coronation, the chair is placed in front of the High Altar of Westminster Abbey. The chair is made of oak, and was made for King Edward I. It was decorated with paintings of birds, animals and leaves and was gilded with gold, but the chair has become worn over the years.

Supporting the chair are four golden lions. The chair has a special shelf under

it where the Scottish Stone of Destiny is placed.

The Stone of Destiny, or Stone of Scone, is made of sandstone and was used to crown Scottish Kings for hundreds of years. When Edward I invaded Scotland in 1296 he took the stone and brought it to England and it was placed under the Coronation Chair in 1307.

FUN FACT: early tourists and choirboys carved their initials into the Coronation Chair.

ILLUSTRATION: the Coronation Chair with Stone of Scone.

CUT-OUTS: two Royal Crowns. TOP is the Imperial State Crown, and BELOW is St. Edward's Crown. **INSTRUCTIONS:** carefully cut out the two crowns, and attach to the headbands on page 11.

This page is the back of the cut-out crowns, and has no additional content.

CUT-OUTS: two Royal Crowns, in different sizes. Just like the larger crowns on page 7, you can cut them out and use in creative ways. Let your imagination run wild! You can see some examples of creative uses on page 43 and the back cover of this book.

This page is the back of the cut-out crowns, and has no additional content.

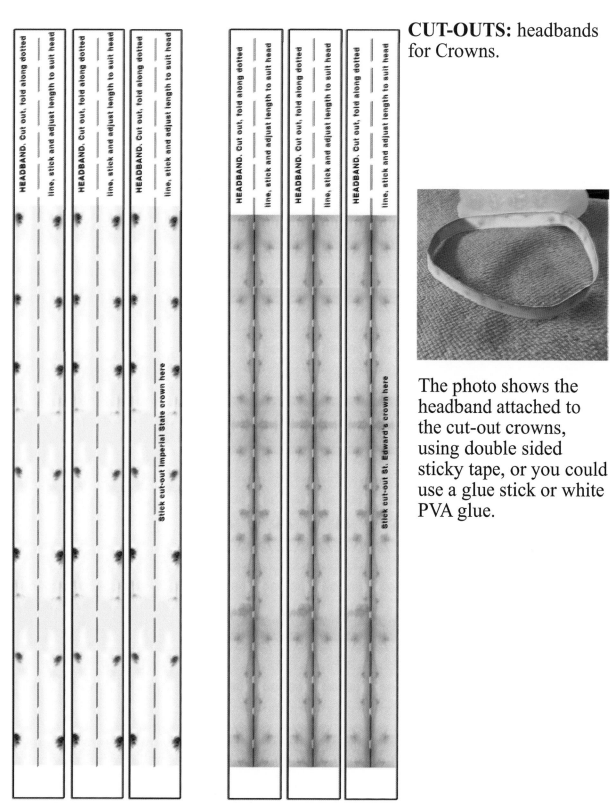

HEADBAND. Cut out, fold along dotted line, stick and adjust length to suit head

HEADBAND. Cut out, fold along dotted line, stick and adjust length to suit head

HEADBAND. Cut out, fold along dotted line, stick and adjust length to suit head

Stick cut-out Imperial State crown here

HEADBAND. Cut out, fold along dotted line, stick and adjust length to suit head

HEADBAND. Cut out, fold along dotted line, stick and adjust length to suit head

HEADBAND. Cut out, fold along dotted line, stick and adjust length to suit head

Stick cut-out St. Edward's crown here

CUT-OUTS: headbands for Crowns.

The photo shows the headband attached to the cut-out crowns, using double sided sticky tape, or you could use a glue stick or white PVA glue.

INSTRUCTIONS: the headbands attach to the Crowns on page 7. Cut out the strips, and fold along the dotted lines, joining sections together to suit head size.

This page is the back of the cut-out headbands, and has no additional content.

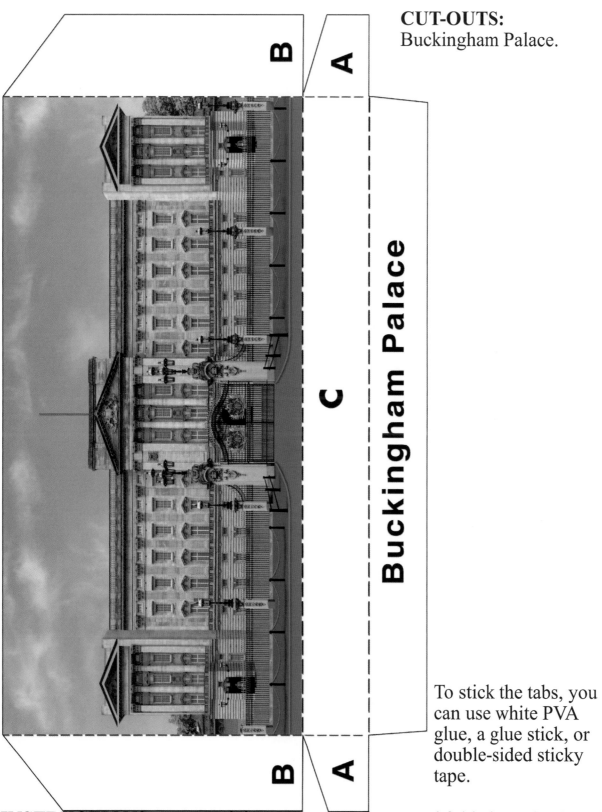

Buckingham Palace

C

B A

B A

To stick the tabs, you can use white PVA glue, a glue stick, or double-sided sticky tape.

INSTRUCTIONS: cut round the outer edges, score and fold along the dotted lines. Double fold Tab C, and stick Tabs A to Tabs B.

This page is the back of the cut-out
Buckingham Palace, and has no additional
content.

Buckingham Palace

Buckingham Palace is a working building and it is the official residence of the reigning British monarch. King Charles III was born in Buckingham Palace. In 1761 George III bought the original house for Queen Charlotte and it was then known as the Queen's House.

During 19th Century the house was enlarged by architects John Nash and Edward Blore, and it became the official residence of Queen Victoria in 1837.

Over the years Kings and Queens living in Buckingham Palace have hosted many state occasions, ranging from banquets, lunches, dinners and receptions, to audiences with Prime Ministers and garden parties.

When open for the public, Buckingham Palace has over 50000 visitors a year.

The Royal Mews is part of Buckingham Palace and is home to the Royal Transport and horses.

FUN FACT: the original house, which was built for the Duke of Buckingham in 1703, was on land that had previously been a mulberry garden planted to feed silkworms.

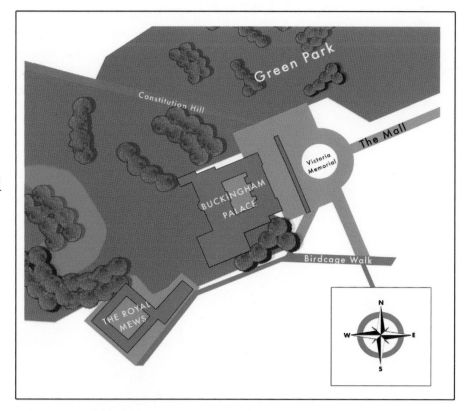

ILLUSTRATION: aerial view of Buckingham Palace and Gardens.

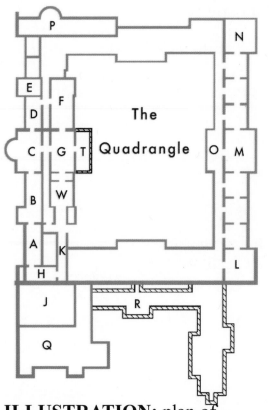

ILLUSTRATION: plan of Buckingham Palace. The rooms are described on this and the next page.

FUN FACT: Buckingham Palace has 775 rooms, 19 state rooms and 78 bathrooms.

A. State Dining Room - This room was completed shortly after Queen Victoria arrived at Buckingham Palace.

B. Blue Drawing Room - Originally used for entertaining. The King uses this room to host receptions.

C. Music Room - This room was completed in 1831 and it was originally known as the Bow Drawing Room, the Music Room was completed in 1831 and has not been altered since. It's a room where some royal babies have been christened including King Charles III.

D. The White Drawing Room - This room dates back to the 1820s, and has some amazing art on its walls. It has a gilded piano which is made of painted and varnished mahogany, satinwood and pine with brass and gilt bronze mounts.

E. The Royal Closet - This was originally known as the Queen's Closet or the Queen's State Audience Room. Now it is simply known as the Royal Closet and it is where the Royal Family gather before state occasions. It also has a cleverly concealed door in the wall, known as a jib door.

F. The Throne Room - This room is used for court ceremonies and official entertaining. There are two throne chairs known, as the Chairs of Estate and they were used at the Coronation of Queen Elizabeth II. The room is a magnificent rich red colour and it was where the Duke and Duchess of Cambridge had their wedding photographs taken.

G. The Green Drawing Room - This room was remodelled for Queen Charlotte and then changed again by John Nash for King George IV. It's called the Green Drawing Room because of the green wall covering.

H. Cross Gallery - This room has a domed ceiling and walls divided into panels and covered in famous paintings.

J. Ball Room - The Ball Room in Buckingham Palace is enormous. It is used for state banquets and investitures and it has a musicians gallery with an organ.

K. East Gallery - This room connects to Queen Victoria's ballroom.

L. Yellow Drawing Room - This room is now used as a meeting room. It is at the west end of the Great Gallery on the first floor of the palace.

M. Centre Balcony Room - This room, which is behind the balcony is a private room. This means that visitors cannot go there. Although it is now called the Balcony Room it was once known as the Chinese Dining Room.

N. Chinese Luncheon Room - This room is furnished in the Chinese Regency style. It's on the first floor of the Palace and has been the setting for a number of portraits of the royal family.

P. Private Apartments - Along the northwest side of the palace towards at the back of Buckingham Palace, there are a number of private apartments. Queen Elizabeth II lived there.

Q. Service Areas

W. The Grand Staircase - Designed by John Nash, this staircase is very grand and very dramatic. It has 34 steps leading up to the Throne Room.

Ground Floor

R. Ambassador's Entrance - When Buckingham Palace was first opened to the public entry was through the Ambassador's Entrance and into a waiting room.

T. Grand Entrance - Guests of the King or Queen enter Buckingham Palace through the Grand Entrance. Heads of State and Prime Ministers enter the palace here and so can you.

"They're changing the guard at Buckingham Palace."

This famous line is part of a verse by A.A.Milne, and was made into a song about the changing of the guard at Buckingham Palace. The ceremony is a favourite attraction for tourists to London, and it regularly happens at 11 a.m. outside the Palace. Different British guards perform the guarding duties, including the Grenadier Guards, the Coldstream Guards, The Scots Guards, The Irish Guards and The Welsh Guards.

The Grenadier Guards

The Grenadier Guards are one of the oldest and most senior regiments in the British Army, and guardsmen are often seen standing guard outside Buckingham Palace.

Their distinctive red uniforms and black bearskins make them readily identifiable. A bearskin is a tall fur cap and is the traditional headgear of a Grenadier guardsman and is made from the fur of Canadian black bears.

The guards don't just perform ceremonial duties, they also guard the King and Queen at night by patrolling the grounds around Buckingham Palace and St. James's Palace.

FUN FACT: the bearskin worn by the Grenadier Guards is 18 inches tall (45.7 cm) and weighs one and a half pounds (0.68 Kg).

ILLUSTRATION: Palace Guard.

CUT-OUTS:

animated guard. You will be able to animate the guard and make him quick march!

To assemble the guard, you will need 4 metal paper fasteners like these:

LEFT　　　　**RIGHT (as viewed from front)**

INSTRUCTIONS: to make your cut-out guard, cut around the body, legs and arms. Push 4 metal paper fasteners, like those illustrated. '+' marks the spot. Attach the arms and legs behind the body.

This page is the back of the cut-out guard, and has no additional content.

Westminster Abbey

Westminster Abbey is an amazing building.

For over 1000 years, people have worshipped, celebrated and attended great ceremonies within its walls. It has been the setting for State occasions, Royal Weddings, Coronations and burials of the great and the good.

Westminster Abbey is built in the shape of a cross. Its full name is the Collegiate Church of Saint Peter at Westminster.

Westminster Abbey is a building which has not always stayed the same. Between 1042 and 1052 Edward the Confessor built the first great building, then in 1245 the church that we see today began to be built.

The Abbey is close to the Houses of Parliament and Big Ben.

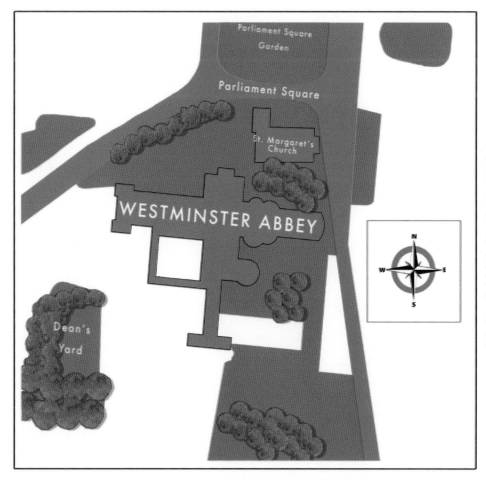

FUN FACT: in 1998, ten statues of modern martyrs were placed in the niches above the Abbey's Great West Door.

ILLUSTRATION: aerial view of Westminster Abbey and surroundings.

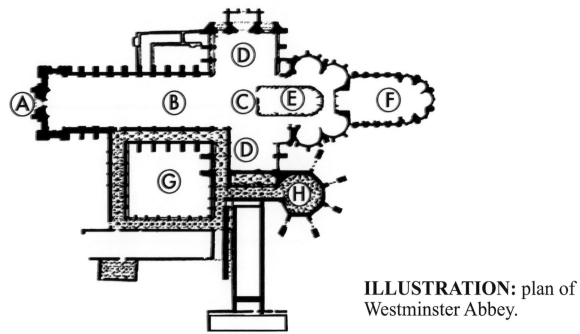

ILLUSTRATION: plan of Westminster Abbey.

A. Great West Door - Main Entrance.

B. Nave - The nave is a central part of a church and is usually rectangular. The nave is at the western end of the Abbey, and many famous people are buried there.

C. Crossing

D. Transepts - The transept is a part of the church which is at right-angles to the knave, making the building in the shape of a cross.

E. Choir - Music has been sung for over 1000 years in this part of the Abbey. The stalls (seats) are set behind a beautiful Quire screen.

F. Henry VII Chapel - The Henry VII Chapel is at the western end of the Abbey. Henry VII paid for the chapel to be built by leaving money in his will. It has three aisles, a nave, an altar and a stunning fan vaulted ceiling.

G. Cloister - A cloister is a covered stone passage and at Westminster Abbey each cloister is about 100 feet long and runs around a courtyard.

H. Chapter House - The Chapter House at Westminster Abbey is in the East Cloister. A Chapter House was a place where monks could meet with the 'Abbot' (the man in charge of the monastery). This Chapter House is octagonal and has a beautiful fan-vaulted ceiling. It is reported to have the oldest door in Britain, dating back to 1050.

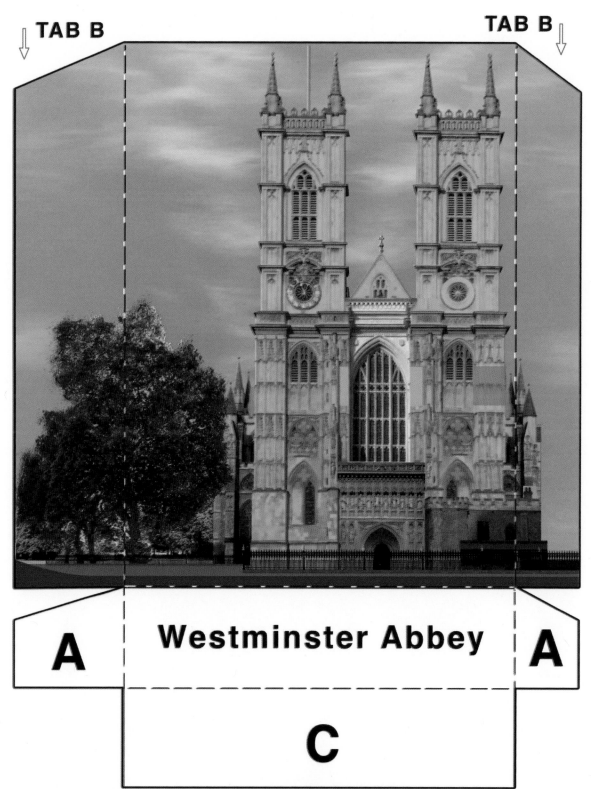

A   **Westminster Abbey**   A

C

CUT-OUTS: Westminster Abbey. **INSTRUCTIONS:** cut round the outer edges, score and fold along the dotted lines. Double fold Tab C, and stick both Tabs A to the bottom of side Tabs B. Use a glue stick, white PVA glue, or double sided sticky tape.

This page is the back of the cut-out of Westminster Abbey, and has no additional content.

Cosmati Pavement

Right in front of the High Altar in Westminster Abbey is special floor which is known as the 'Cosmati Pavement', and it plays a special role in the Coronation. It is where Kings and Queens have been crowned for over 700 years, sitting on the Coronation Chair.

The Cosmati Pavement was commissioned by Henry III and completed in 1268. The pavement is made of marble, stone, glass and metal. All the pieces are put together in a magnificent pattern or mosaic.

The types of stone used are onyx, purple porphyry, green serpentine and yellow limestone together with red, turquoise, cobalt blue and bluish white glass.

From the 1870s, The Cosmati Pavement was hidden under carpet. It is 7m 58 cm (24 foot 10 inch) square.

ILLUSTRATION: Cosmati Pavement.

FUN FACT: the pavement is made of over 80,000 pieces of stone.

COLOURING & DRAWING: designs inspired by The Cosmati Pavement. 5 designs to colour, and have a go at designing your own in the blank shape.

The Diamond Jubilee State Coach
(Illustrated LEFT)

The Diamond Jubilee State Coach is a very modern coach. It was built in Australia for Queen Elizabeth II's Diamond Jubilee celebrating her 60 year reign. The coach weighs over 3 tonnes and needs 6 horses to pull it.

The Coach holds a few surprises. It has an aluminium body and up-to-date suspension to stop it from swaying too much. When the coach was built, the panels and windows used wood from many of Britain's historic sites and organisations. Materials came from Canterbury Cathedral, Henry VIII's flagship, the 'Mary Rose', the Antarctic bases of Captain Scott and Ernest Shackleton, and Balmoral Castle. There is even a fragment from Florence Nightingale's dress. The seat handrails are from the Royal Yacht Britannia and the coach even has heating, electric windows and air conditioning. The Jubilee State Coach has a huge gold crown on the top which was carved from oak from HMS Victory.

 FUN FACT: the gilded crown on the top of the Diamond Jubilee State Coach holds a secret. It has a camera to film the journey!

The Gold State Coach (Cut-Out Model on pages 29-35)

The Gold State Coach is over 260 years old, and is drawn by eight Windsor Grey horses. It has been used for every coronation since 1831. The Gold State Coach isn't made of solid gold but of gilded wood. It is 7m long, 3.6m tall and weighs 4 tonnes. Around the coach are Giovanni Battista Cipriani's painted panels of Roman Gods and Goddesses, and on the top of the roof are three cherubs carrying the Imperial Crown and holding a sword, sceptre and badge representing knighthood. The coach is covered with rich carvings with tritons on each corner, lion's heads and gilded dolphins.

When the coach was first used it was driven by a coachman. For the Coronation, it will be pulled by a team of eight horses and ridden by four postillions. A postillion is a person who guides a horse-drawn carriage. The grooms operate the breaks on the heavy coach. The Gold State Coach is not particularly comfortable and tends to rock from side to side, and King William IV said it was like being on board a ship 'tossing in a rough sea'.

ILLUSTRATION: some of the completed models.

1.

2. **3.** **4.** **5.**

1. The completed model of the Gold State Coach. The horses with postillions (riders) attach to the left-hand side, and the horses without riders go on the right-hand side (as shown).

2. & 3. The supports attached to give the coach and horses extra stability. To stick the supports, use double-sided tape, a glue stick, or white PVA glue.

4. Close-up of the finished groom model, showing it free-standing.

5. Detail of the back of the Westminster Abbey cut-out.

INSTRUCTIONS: for the model of the Gold State Coach, see pages 31 and 33.

FUN FACT: Windsor Grey horses were named after 'Windsor', where they were kept in Victorian times. They are at least 16.1 hands (1.65m) high at the withers (the ridge between the shoulder bones).

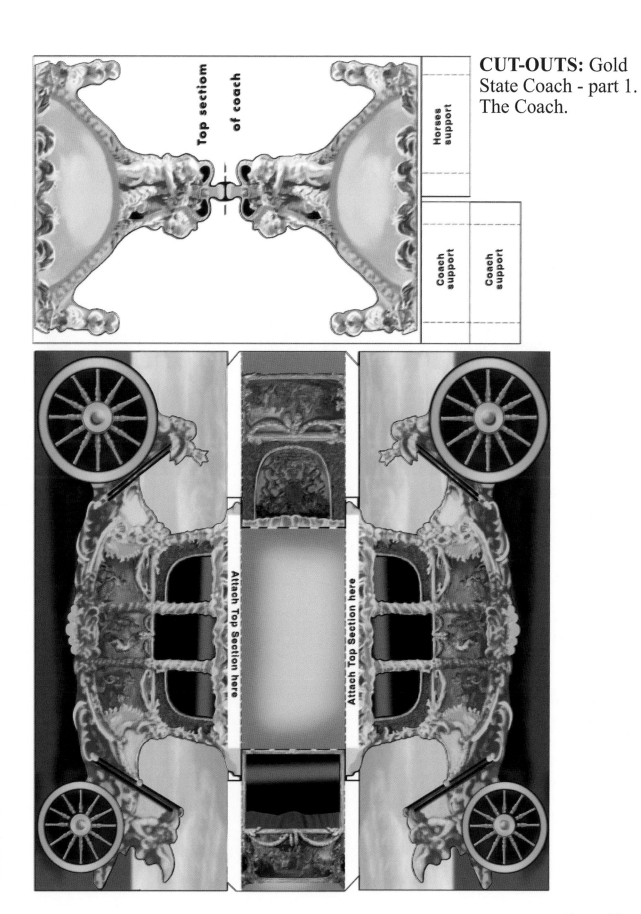

CUT-OUTS: Gold State Coach - part 1. The Coach.

Top section of coach

Horses support

Coach support

Coach support

Attach Top Section here

Attach Top Section here

This page is the back of the cut-out of the Gold State Coach, and has no additional content.

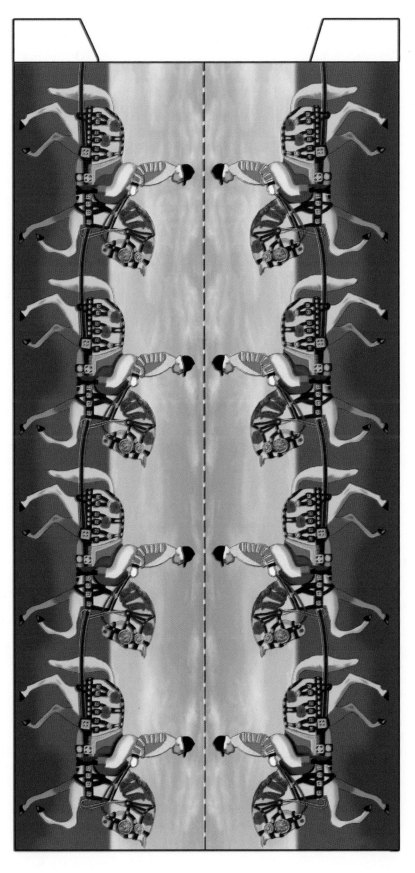

CUT-OUTS: Gold State Coach - part 2. Horses with postillions.

INSTRUCTIONS: to make the model of the Gold State Coach (pages 29-33), cut around the outer lines of the coach on page 29. The top part of of the coach is separate and needs to be cut out, folded in half and attached to the sides of the coach. Cut around the shape with the horses and riders (postillions) and attach to the left-hand side of the coach when viewed from above. Do the same with the horses without riders on page 33.They attach to the right-hand side of the coach. Use the parts marked 'Coach Support' and 'Horses Support' to give the model more stability, as shown in the photographs on page 28. Use a glue stick, white PVA glue, or double sided sticky tape, to attach the parts.

This page is the back of the cut-out of the horses and postillions for the Gold State Coach, and has no additional content.

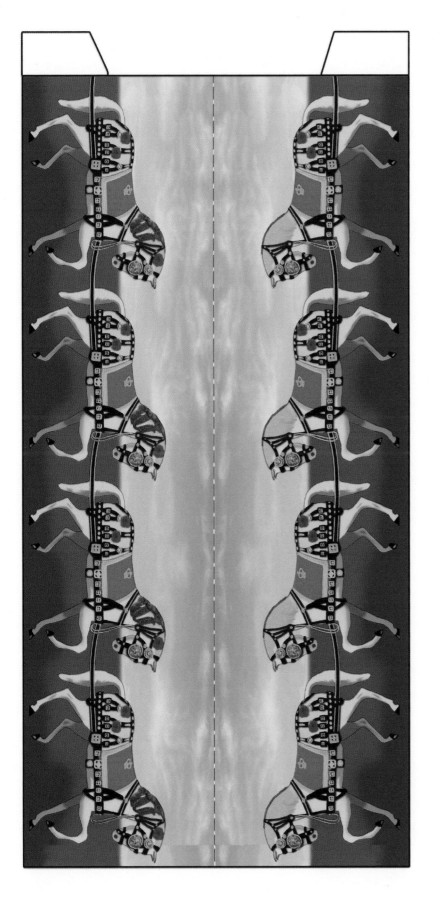

CUT-OUTS: Gold State Coach - part 3. Horses without postillions. For Gold State Coach.

This page is the back of the cut-outs of the horses for the Gold State Coach, and has no additional content.

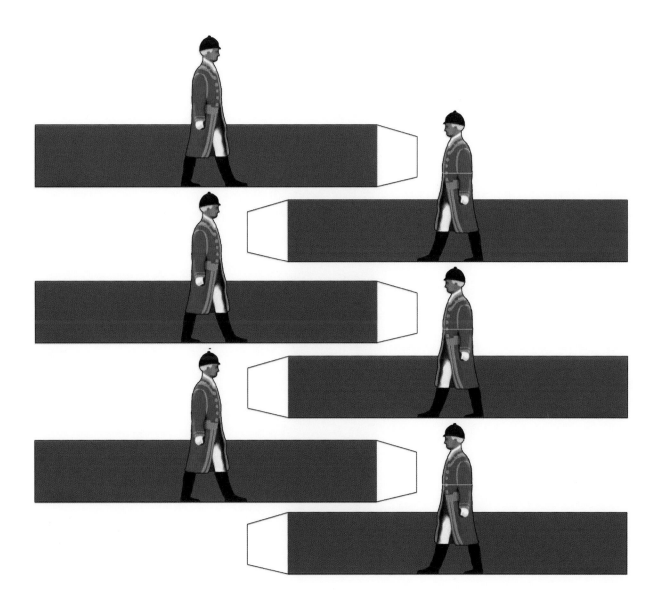

INSTRUCTIONS: carefully cut round the figure and the 'road'. Make the 'road' into a circle, so that the figure can stand up. The grooms and escorts walk alongside the coach and horses. You can see a photo of the completed model on page 28.

This page is the back of the cut-outs of the grooms/escorts the Gold State Coach, and has no additional content.

Fun With Flags

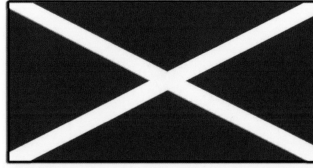

On Coronation Day there will be many flags flying. Flags are flown as symbols of pride and belonging, celebrating the United Kingdom and the Coronation. The Union Flag, or the Union Jack, is the national flag of the United Kingdom. It is the most important of all British flags.

It is call the Union Flag because it is made from three flags of the nations that make up the United Kingdom.

If you separate out all the parts of the Union Jack, you can see flags of three Nations, illustrated LEFT.

At the top, there is the flag of St. George which is England's national flag. It is a red cross on a white background.

Below that, there is St. Andrew's Cross, or the Saltire Cross, which is the national flag of Scotland. It is blue with a white diagonal cross.

The third flag is St. Patrick's Flag, the national flag of Northern Ireland. It has a red diagonal cross on a white background.

 FUN FACT: the first flag representing Britain, in 1606, was known as the 'British Flag' or 'Flag of Britain'.

1.

2.

3.

ILLUSTRATION: creative ways to use the some of the cut-outs in this book. **1.** The Rocking Horse, called *Ascot*, has reins and mane decorated with small triangular flags. **2.** The cuddly toys are holding the larger flags mounted on straws. **3.** The tasty coffee and walnut cake is decorated with small flags on a string, plus there is a cut-out crown stuck to ribbon.

CUT-OUTS: Union Flags (Union Jacks).

INSTRUCTIONS: the two flags here have been turned on their sides to fit the page. Cut around the outside of the two flags. Fold the flag around a paper straw (There is a dotted line to guide where to fold). Stick the two halves, back-to-back, using a glue stick, white PVA glue or double sided sticky tape.

When completed, will have two flags which can been viewed from both sides.

On page 38, you can see two cuddly toys holding the finished flags.

This page is the back of the cut-outs of the larger flags, and has no additional content.

CUT-OUTS: smaller flags

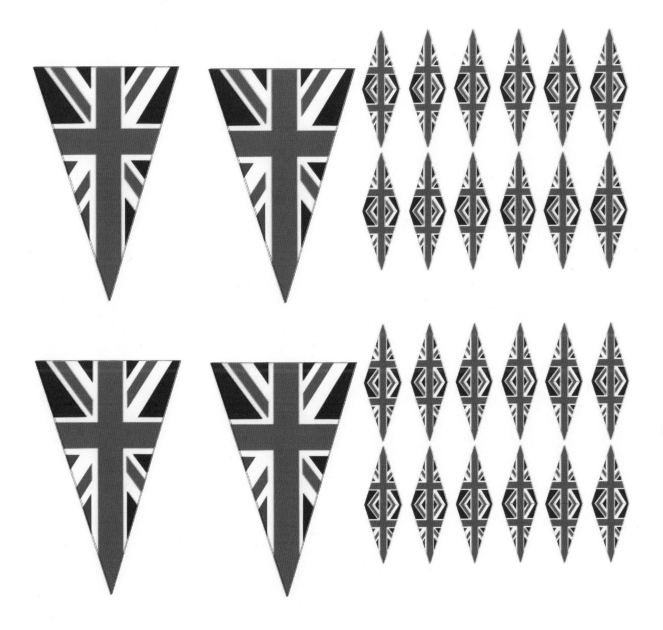

INSTRUCTIONS: cut around the outside of the flags. Attach the larger flags to a length of string. Score and fold the smaller flags along the dotted line, and fold over a length of cotton. Stick the little flags, back-to-back, using a glue stick, white PVA glue, or double sided sticky tape. We have used the little flags to decorate a Coronation cake in the photo on page 38.

This page is the back of the cut-outs of the smaller flags, and has no additional content.

ILLUSTRATION: you can see the fun we have had with the cut-out crowns. We even made our fluffy lion the 'King of the Jungle'! Who would you like to crown a King or Queen?

Bonus Nuggets

I hope you have had fun with this book, and that you are feeling really creative. Creativity is something that is in all of us, but it is a skill that may need coaxing out, and just needs training, practice and refinement.

Many neighbourhoods hold parties around times of celebration. Sometimes parties are held outside in the street, with good food, music and plenty of flags. Of course it is important to let your friends know about the party, so they don't miss out on the fun, and if you and your family are holding a party you can cut out and send the invitations on the next page to your special friends. You could also use them for your next birthday party.

On the covers you can how some of the models in this book will look when you have finished making them. A word about scale. All models are built to scale, which is the ratio of the size of the model to the size of the real object. For instance, the model of the guard on page 19 is approximately 22 cm tall, whereas the real guard would be around 6 feet tall (over 182 cm). This works out as a ratio of approximately 1/8. To fit into the book, the buildings are made to a different scale, because to the same a 1/8 scale as the guard, the Buckingham Palace model would need a piece of paper bigger than a room!

I would like to thank freelance writer, Mhairi Campbell, for all her help in compiling this book. Her knowledge and commitment have been most valuable and helpful.

Jeff Link, April 2023.

Email: norfolknuggets@icloud.com

CUT-OUTS: Party Invitations. **INSTRUCTIONS:** cut out each invitation, and send to your special friends to invite them to your next party.

This page is the back of the cut-outs of the invitations, and has no additional content.

Printed in Great Britain
by Amazon

22290141R00027